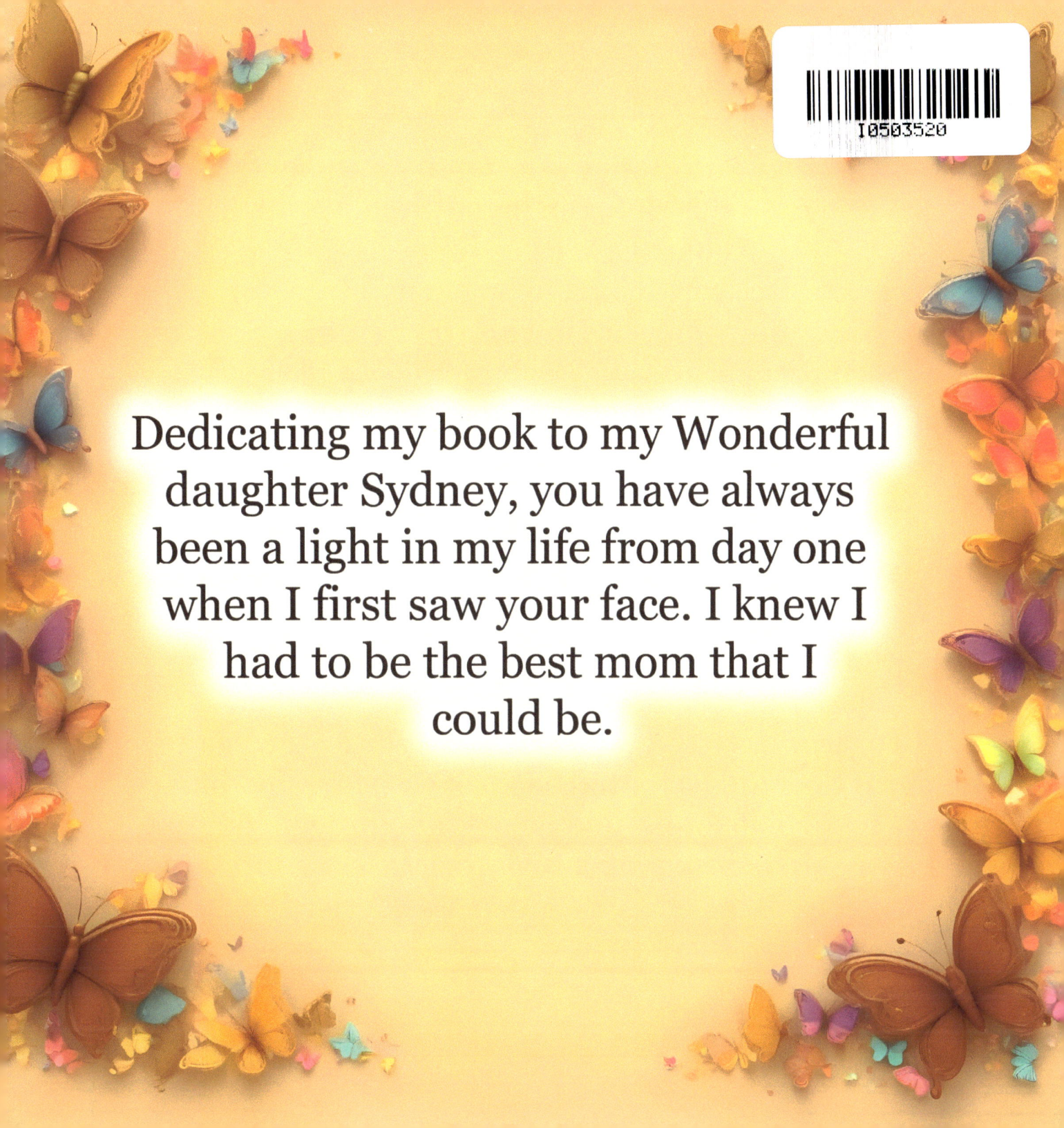

Dedicating my book to my Wonderful daughter Sydney, you have always been a light in my life from day one when I first saw your face. I knew I had to be the best mom that I could be.

Olivia couldn't wait to get out of school for the summer so she could run in the meadow with her dog. Olivia is a spirited little girl with jet-black curly hair and braces on her teeth, with shiny, shiny lips full of strawberry lip gloss and round glasses with butterflies at the top of her frames. Her dad made them for her. She filled her days with wonder and adventure. She lived on a cozy countryside, at the edge of a sprawling meadow in Dacula, GA, with her dog, Polo. Olivia and Polo spent hours chasing butterflies; she was always amazed by their sharp colors and delicate wings.Her fascination with these fluttering creatures began when she was much younger,and it only grew stronger as she learned more about their life cycles and habits. Olivia loved nothing more than for her and Polo to run through the fields, her laughter heard along with the soft rustling of the grass, as butterflies danced around her. As Polo barked, it was like a vivid, swirling ballet.

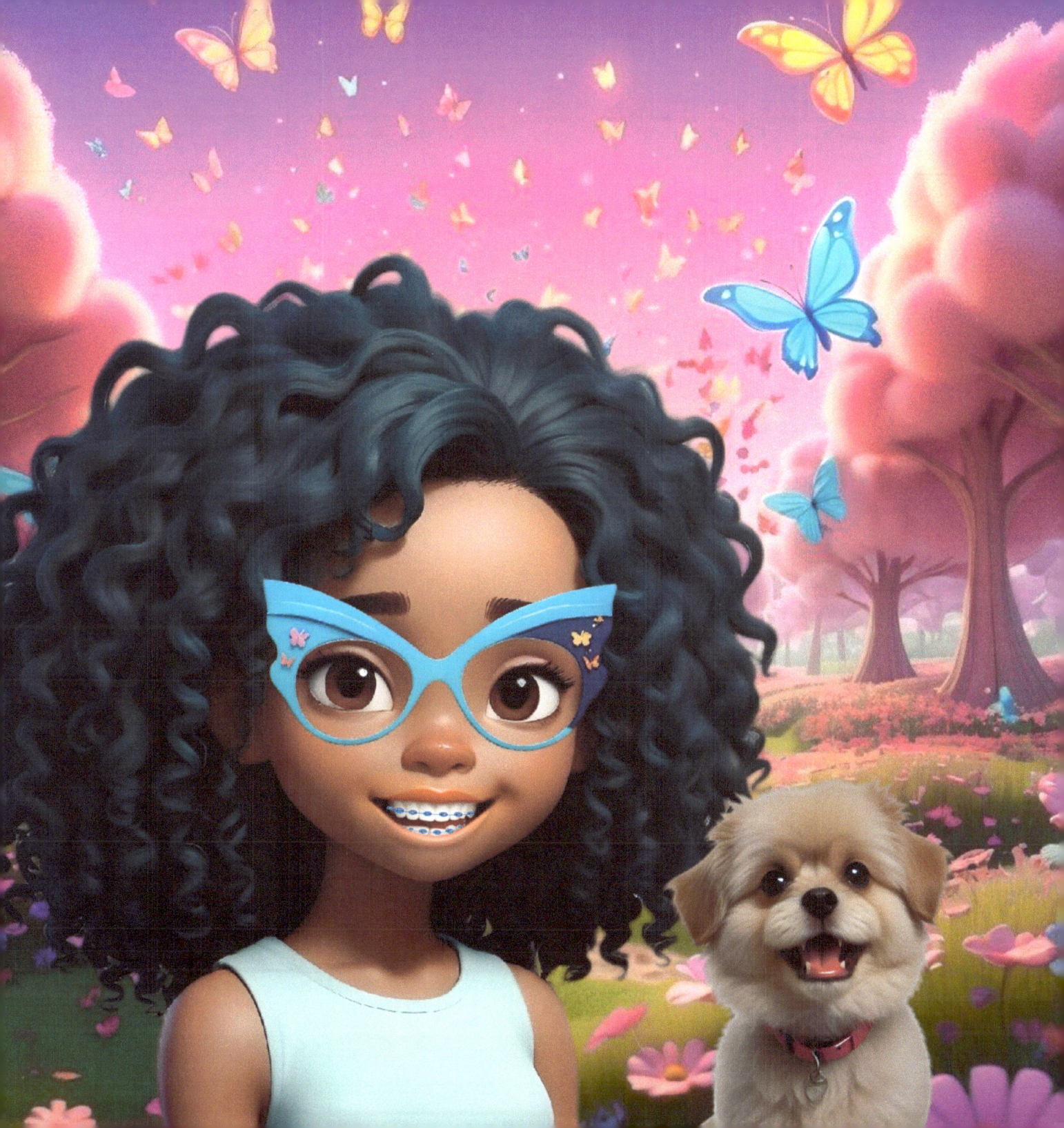

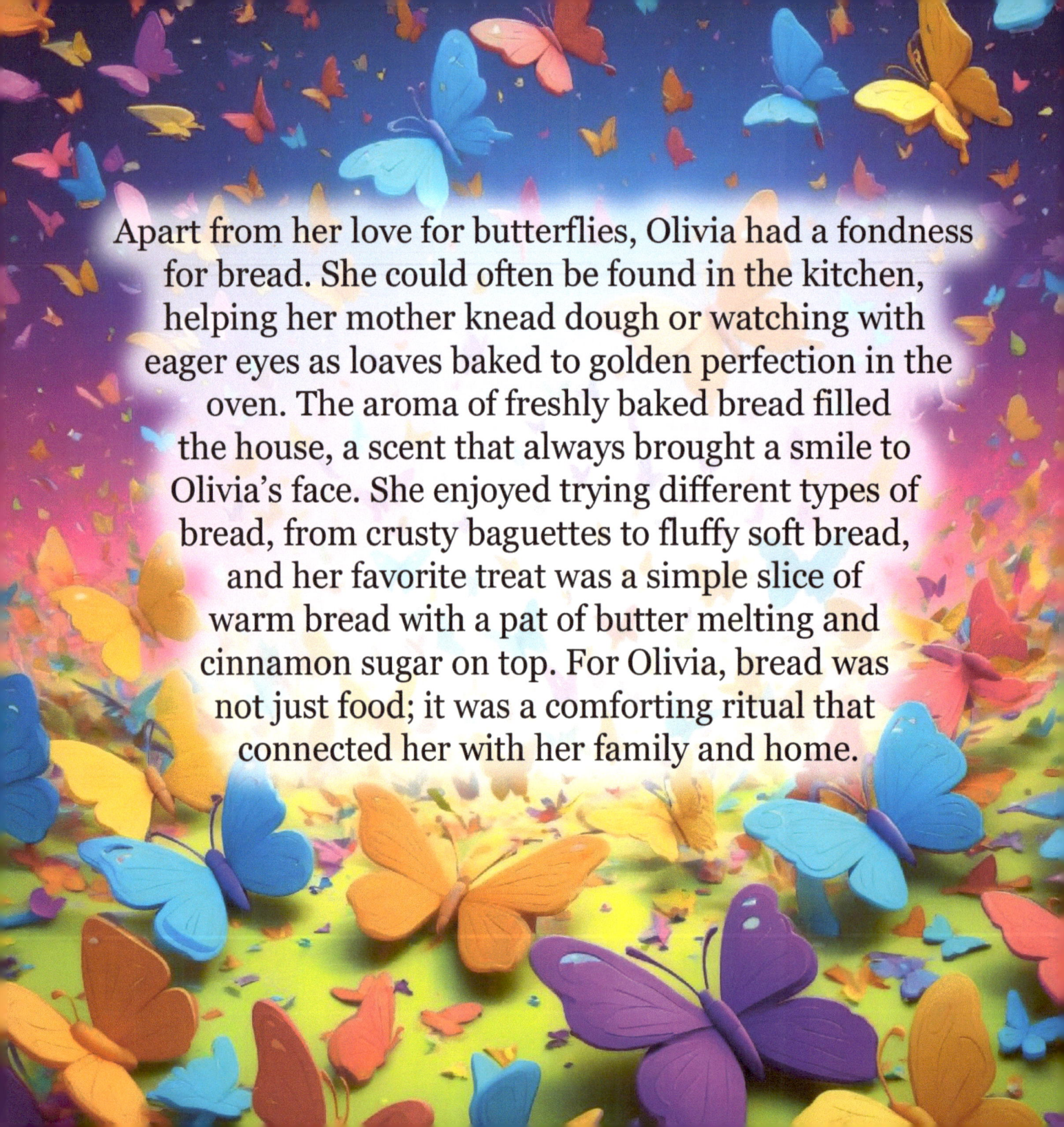

Apart from her love for butterflies, Olivia had a fondness for bread. She could often be found in the kitchen, helping her mother knead dough or watching with eager eyes as loaves baked to golden perfection in the oven. The aroma of freshly baked bread filled the house, a scent that always brought a smile to Olivia's face. She enjoyed trying different types of bread, from crusty baguettes to fluffy soft bread, and her favorite treat was a simple slice of warm bread with a pat of butter melting and cinnamon sugar on top. For Olivia, bread was not just food; it was a comforting ritual that connected her with her family and home.

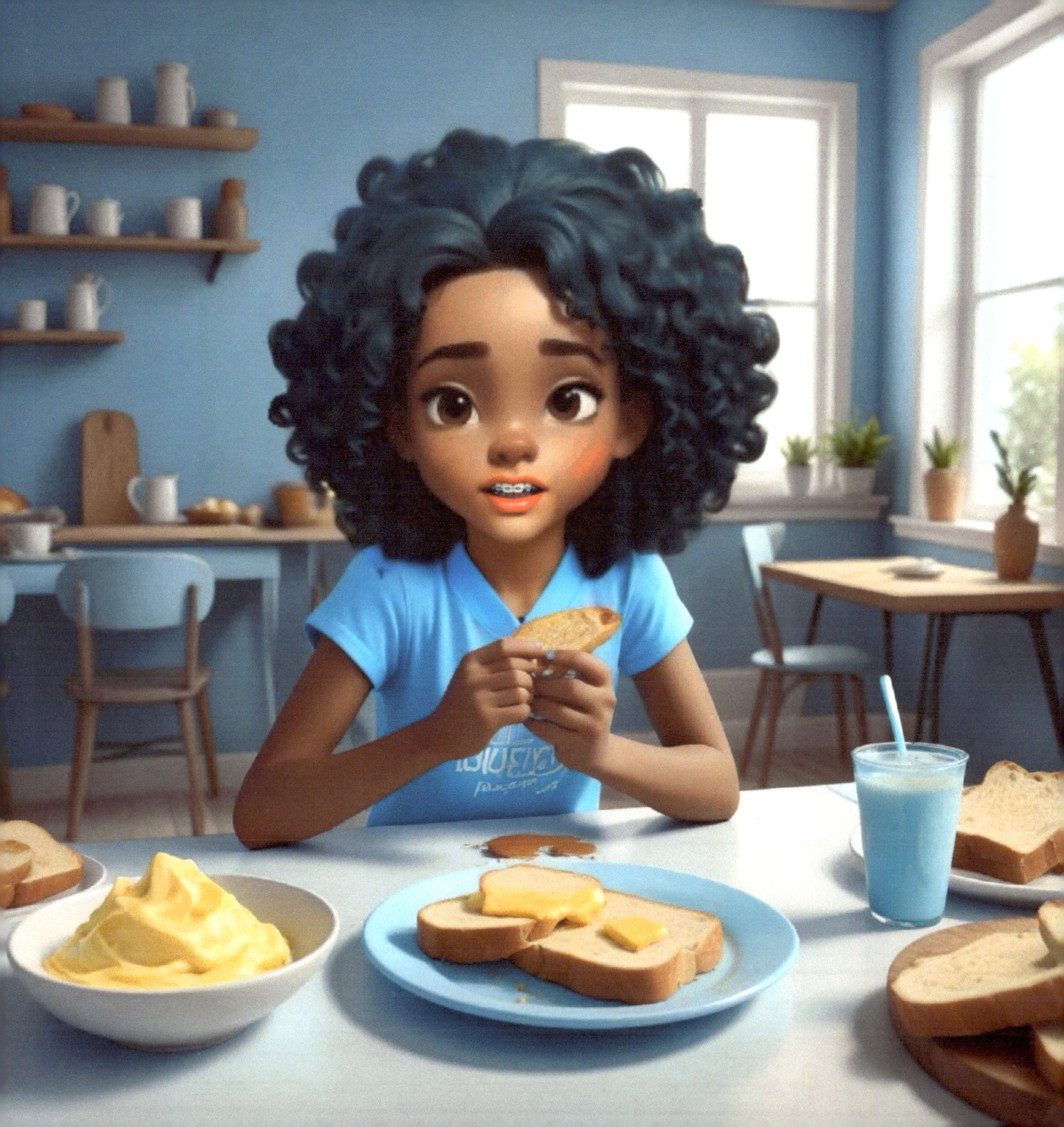

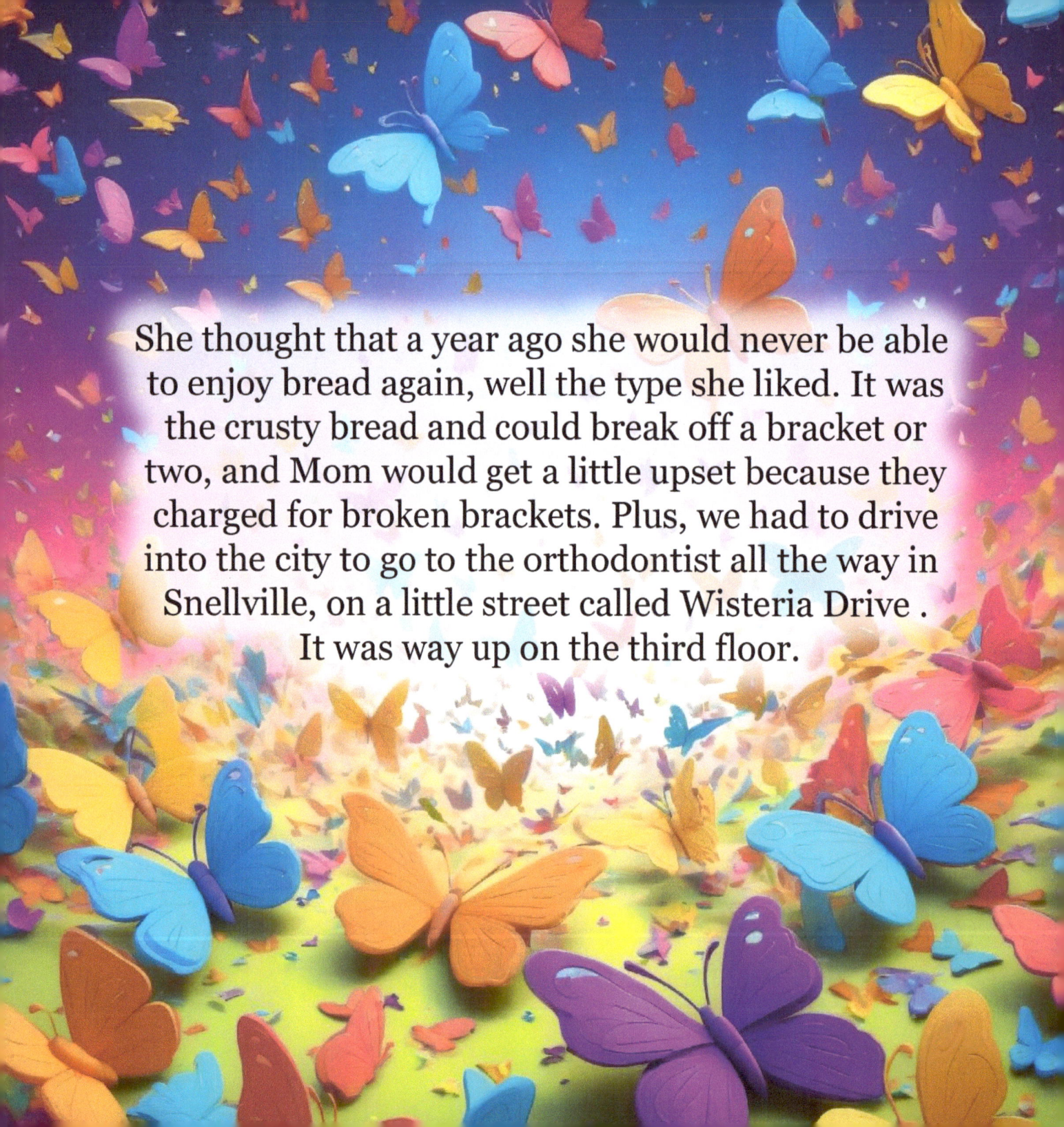

She thought that a year ago she would never be able to enjoy bread again, well the type she liked. It was the crusty bread and could break off a bracket or two, and Mom would get a little upset because they charged for broken brackets. Plus, we had to drive into the city to go to the orthodontist all the way in Snellville, on a little street called Wisteria Drive . It was way up on the third floor.

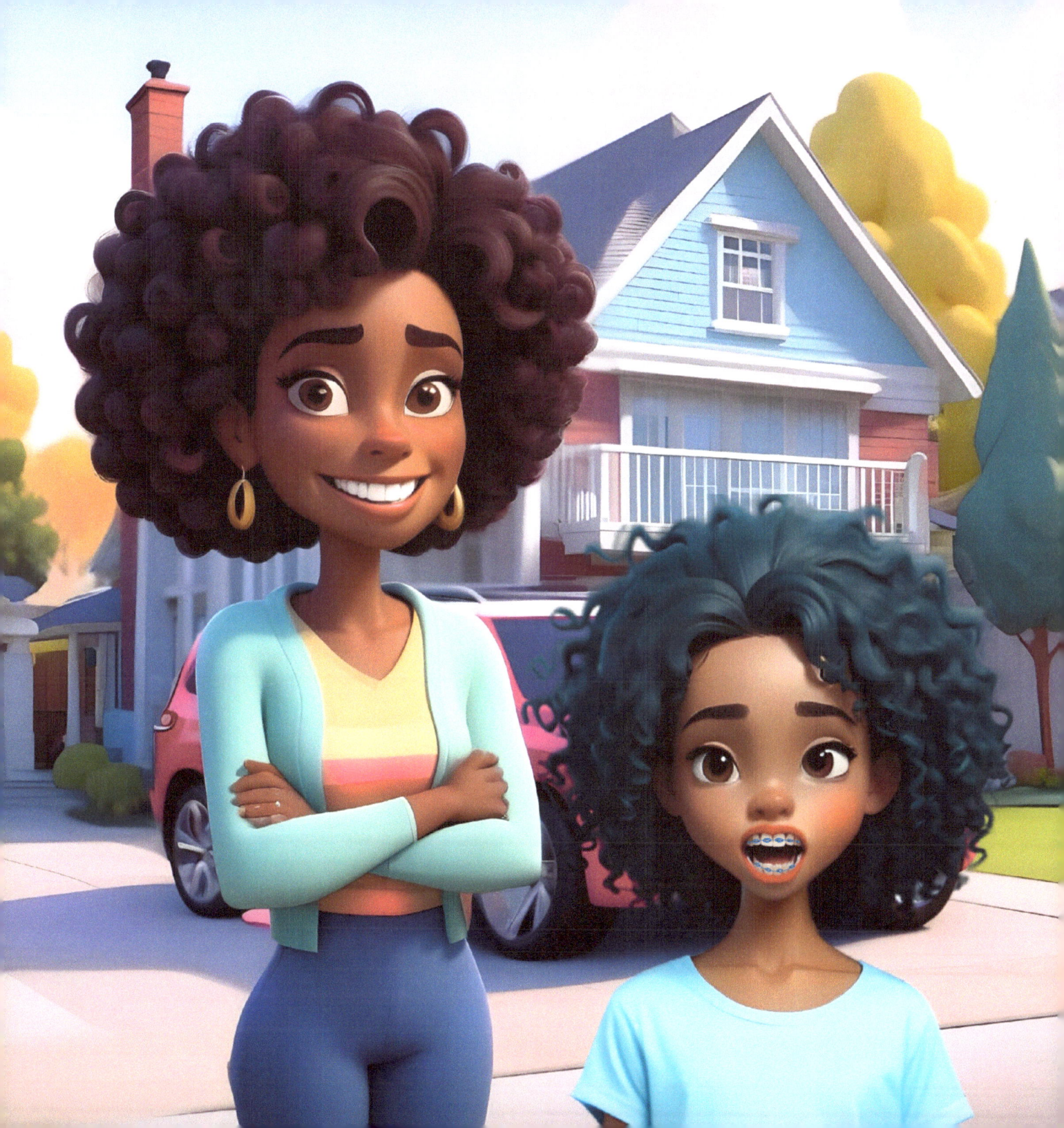

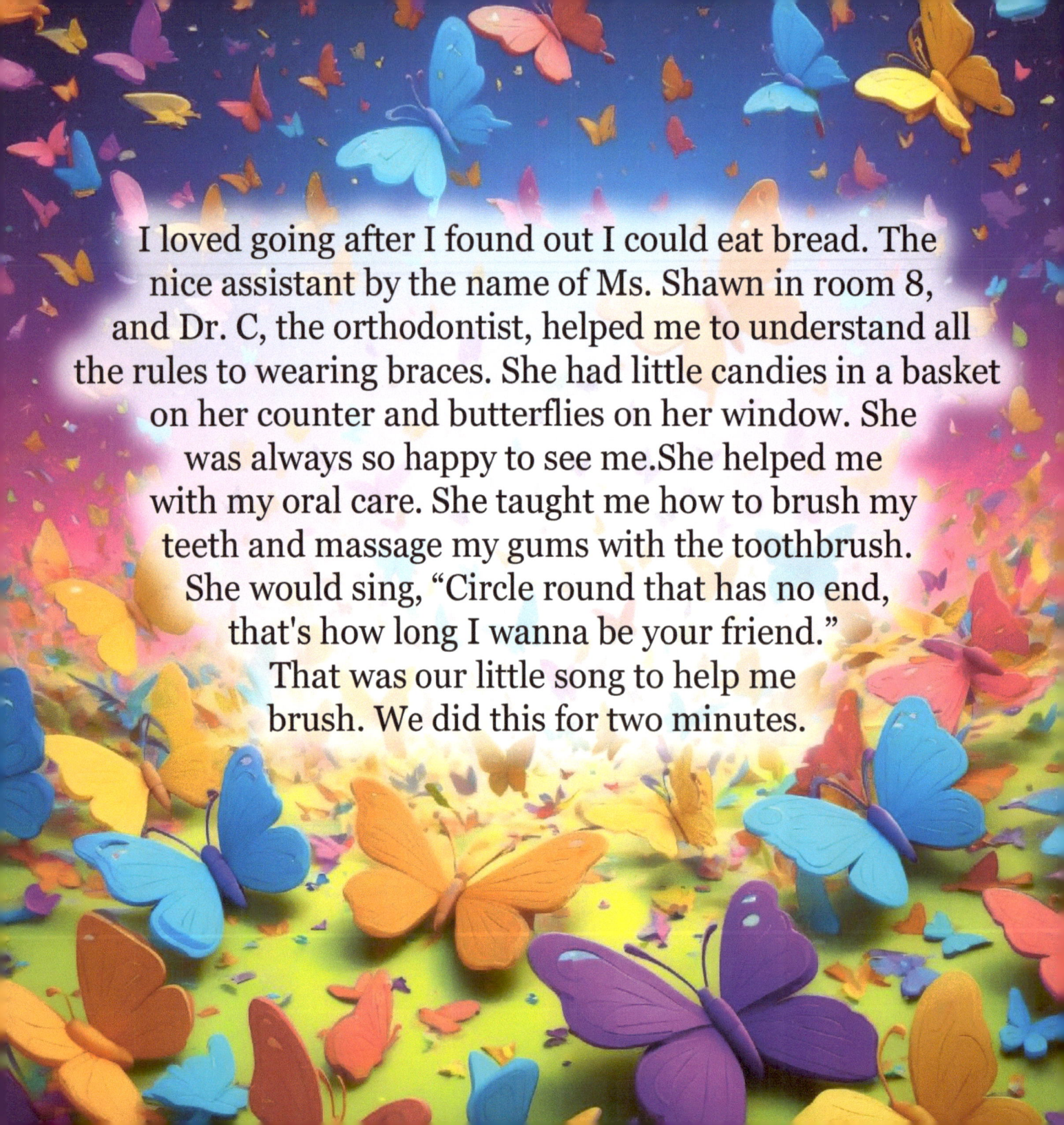

I loved going after I found out I could eat bread. The nice assistant by the name of Ms. Shawn in room 8, and Dr. C, the orthodontist, helped me to understand all the rules to wearing braces. She had little candies in a basket on her counter and butterflies on her window. She was always so happy to see me.She helped me with my oral care. She taught me how to brush my teeth and massage my gums with the toothbrush. She would sing, "Circle round that has no end, that's how long I wanna be your friend." That was our little song to help me brush. We did this for two minutes.

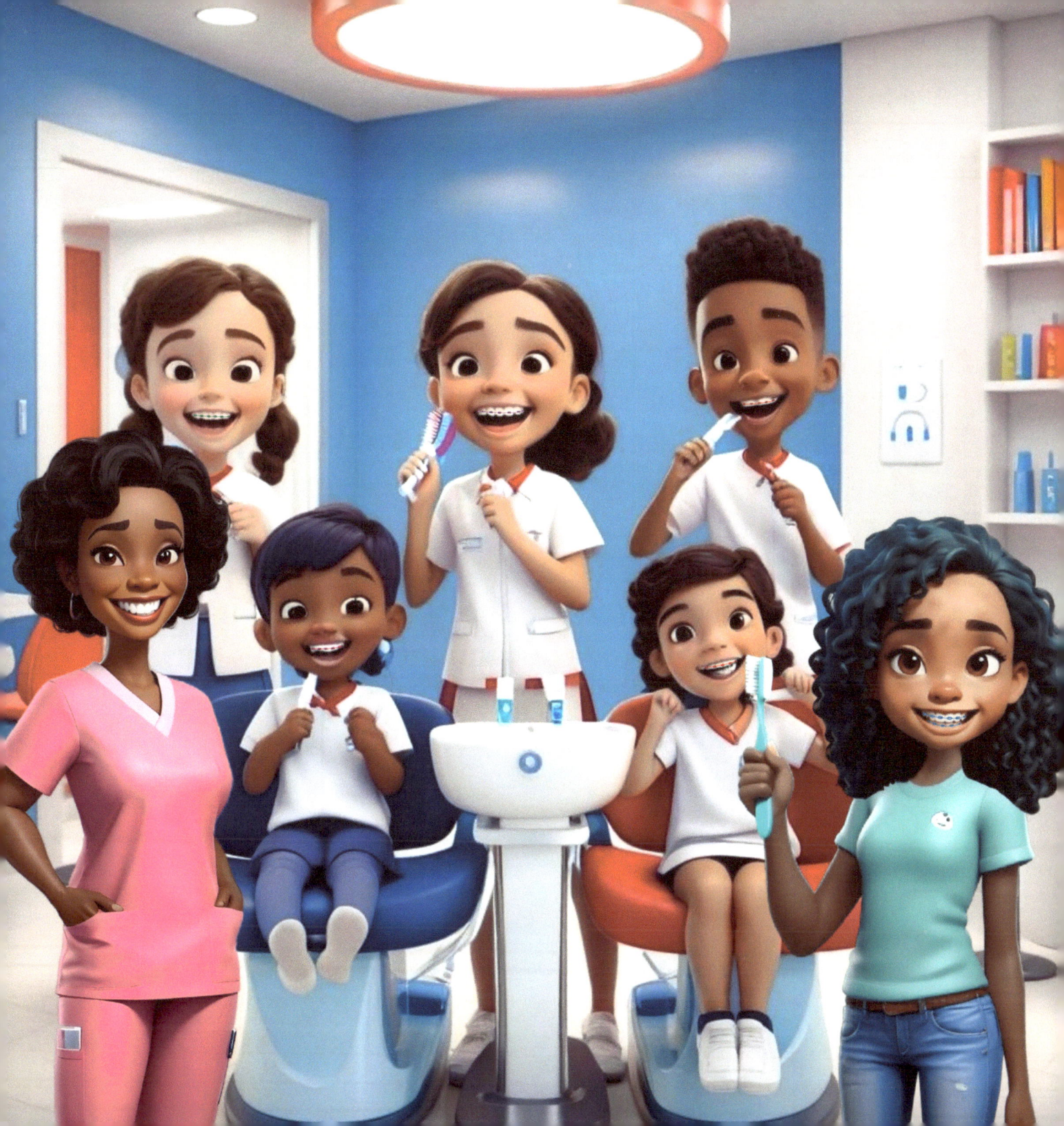

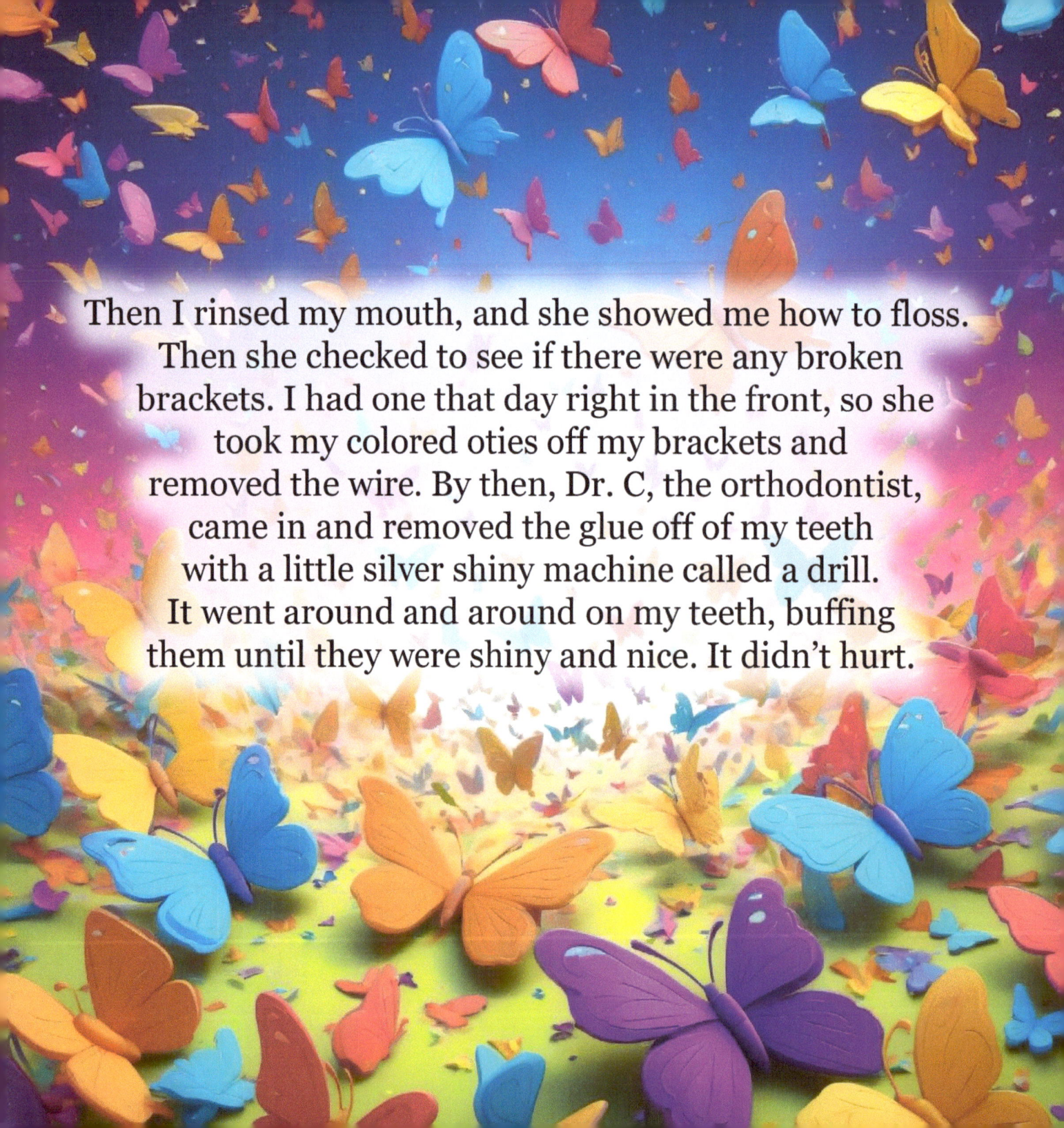

Then I rinsed my mouth, and she showed me how to floss. Then she checked to see if there were any broken brackets. I had one that day right in the front, so she took my colored oties off my brackets and removed the wire. By then, Dr. C, the orthodontist, came in and removed the glue off of my teeth with a little silver shiny machine called a drill. It went around and around on my teeth, buffing them until they were shiny and nice. It didn't hurt.

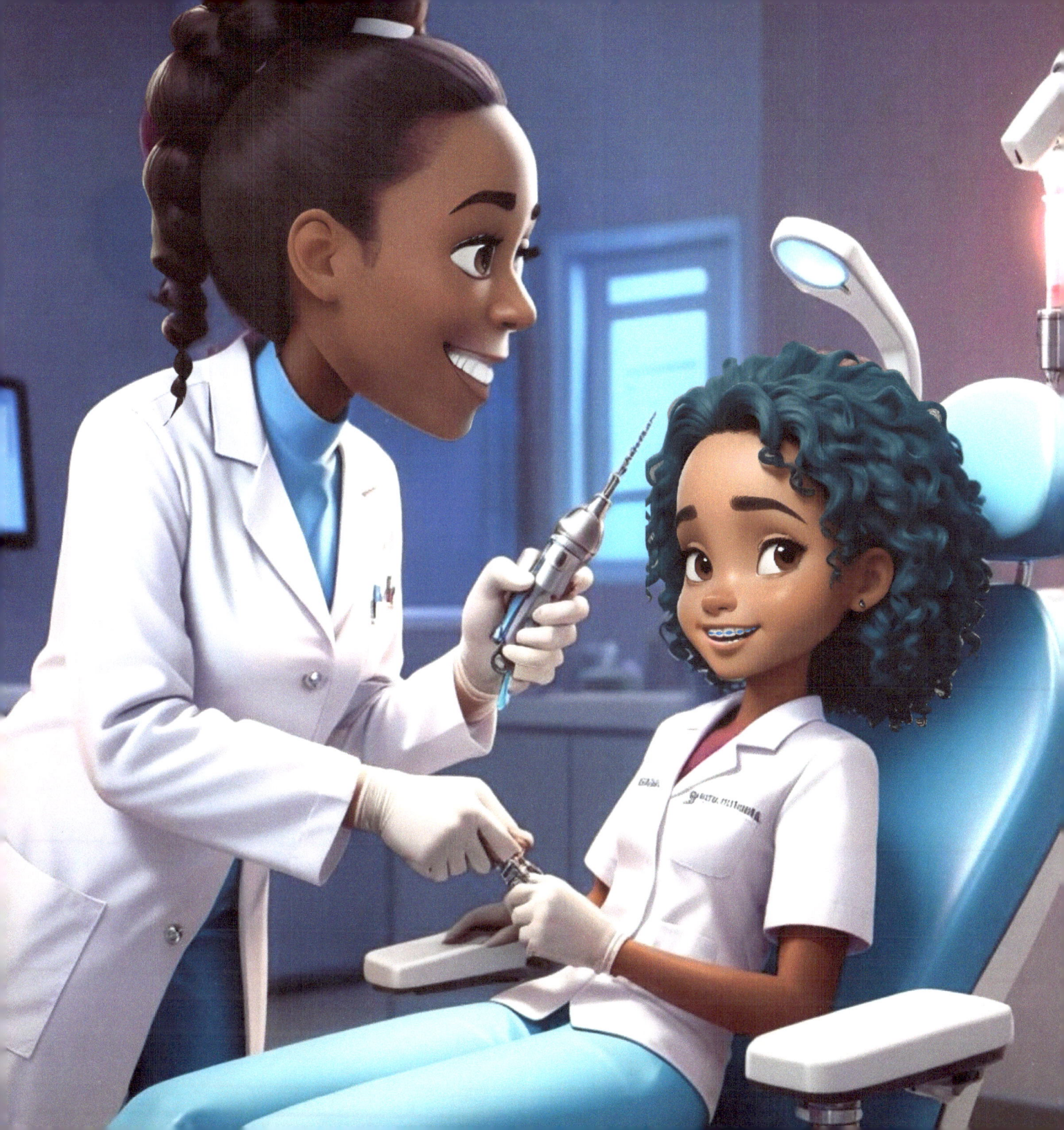

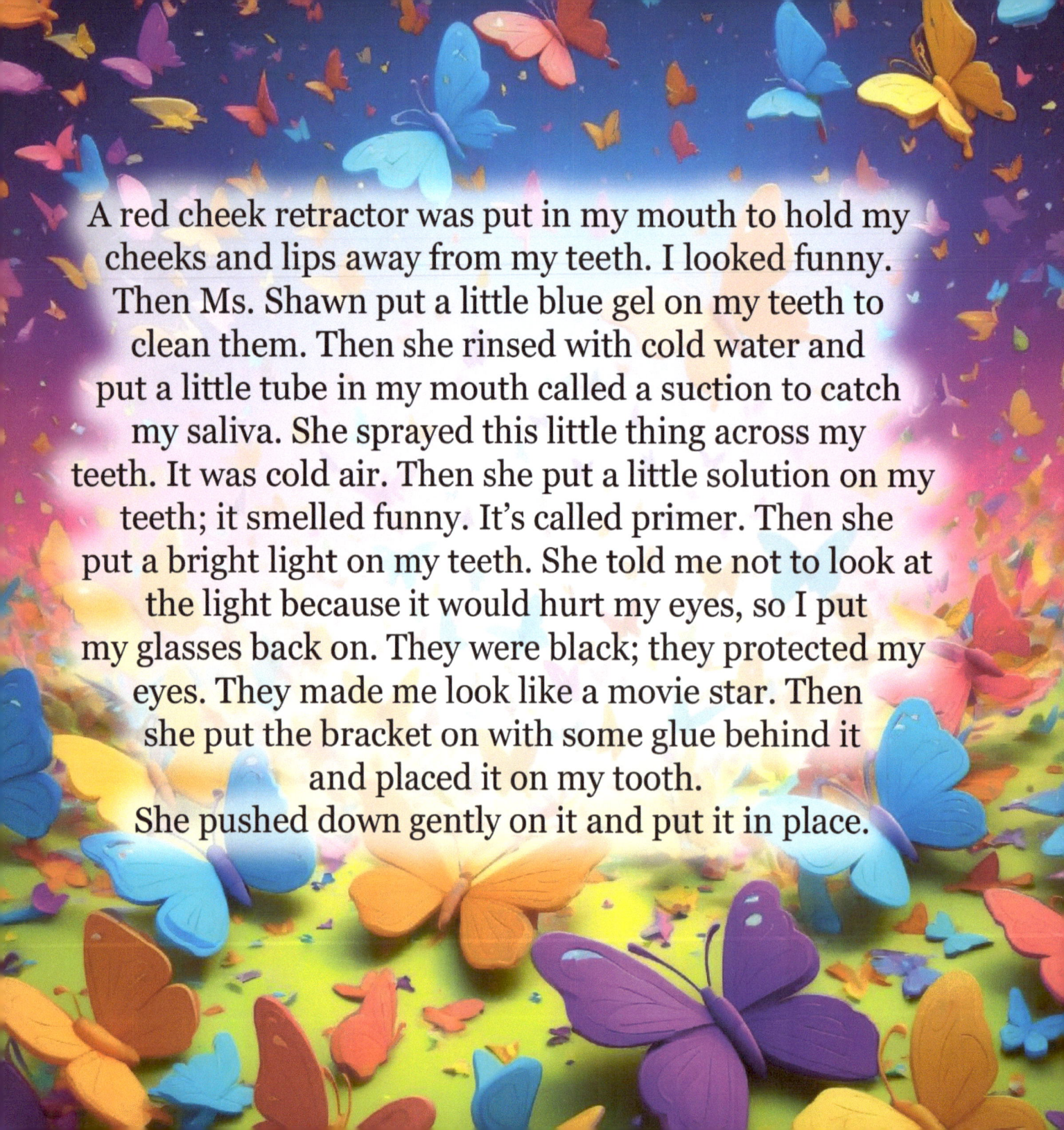

A red cheek retractor was put in my mouth to hold my cheeks and lips away from my teeth. I looked funny. Then Ms. Shawn put a little blue gel on my teeth to clean them. Then she rinsed with cold water and put a little tube in my mouth called a suction to catch my saliva. She sprayed this little thing across my teeth. It was cold air. Then she put a little solution on my teeth; it smelled funny. It's called primer. Then she put a bright light on my teeth. She told me not to look at the light because it would hurt my eyes, so I put my glasses back on. They were black; they protected my eyes. They made me look like a movie star. Then she put the bracket on with some glue behind it and placed it on my tooth.
She pushed down gently on it and put it in place.

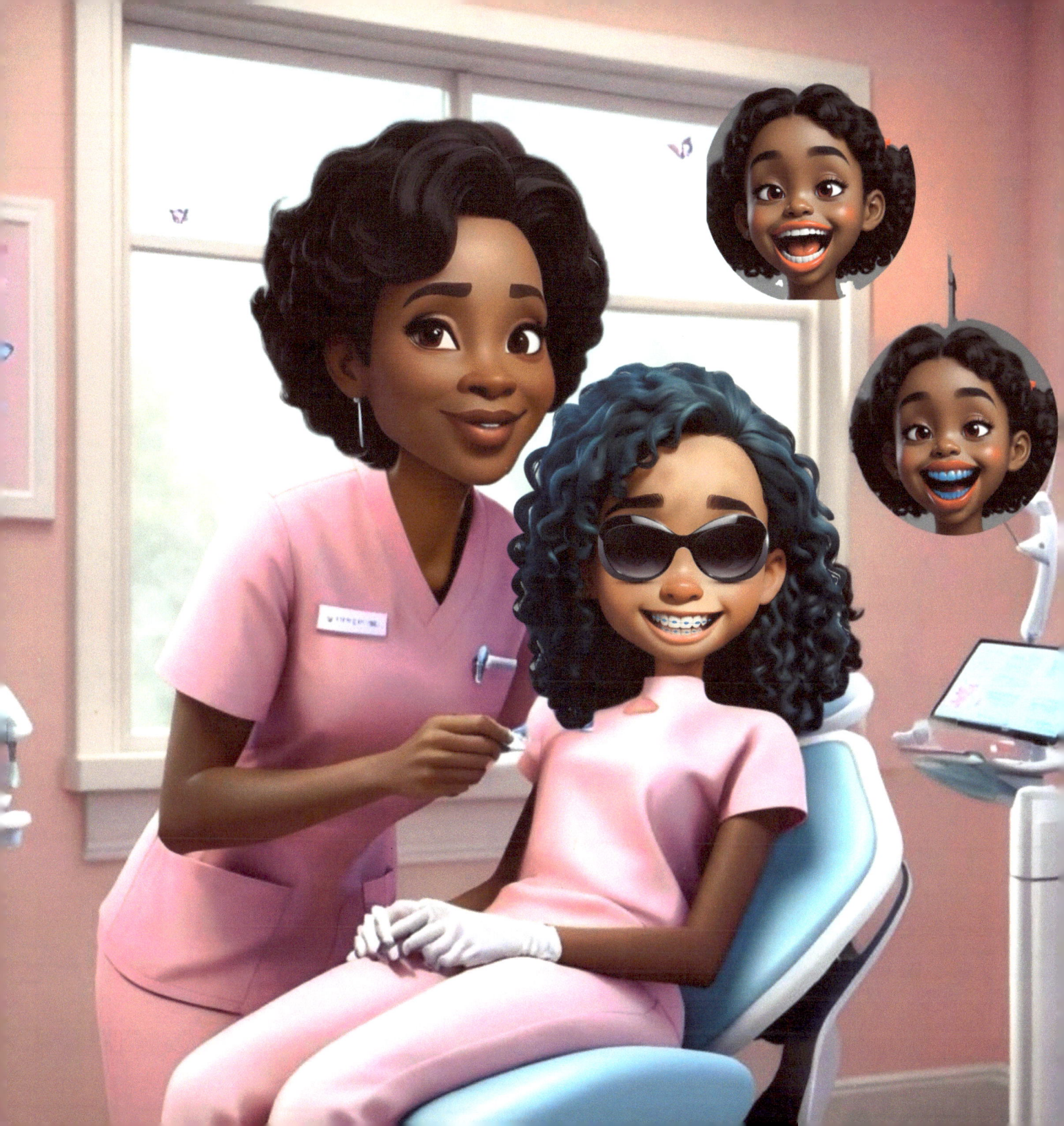

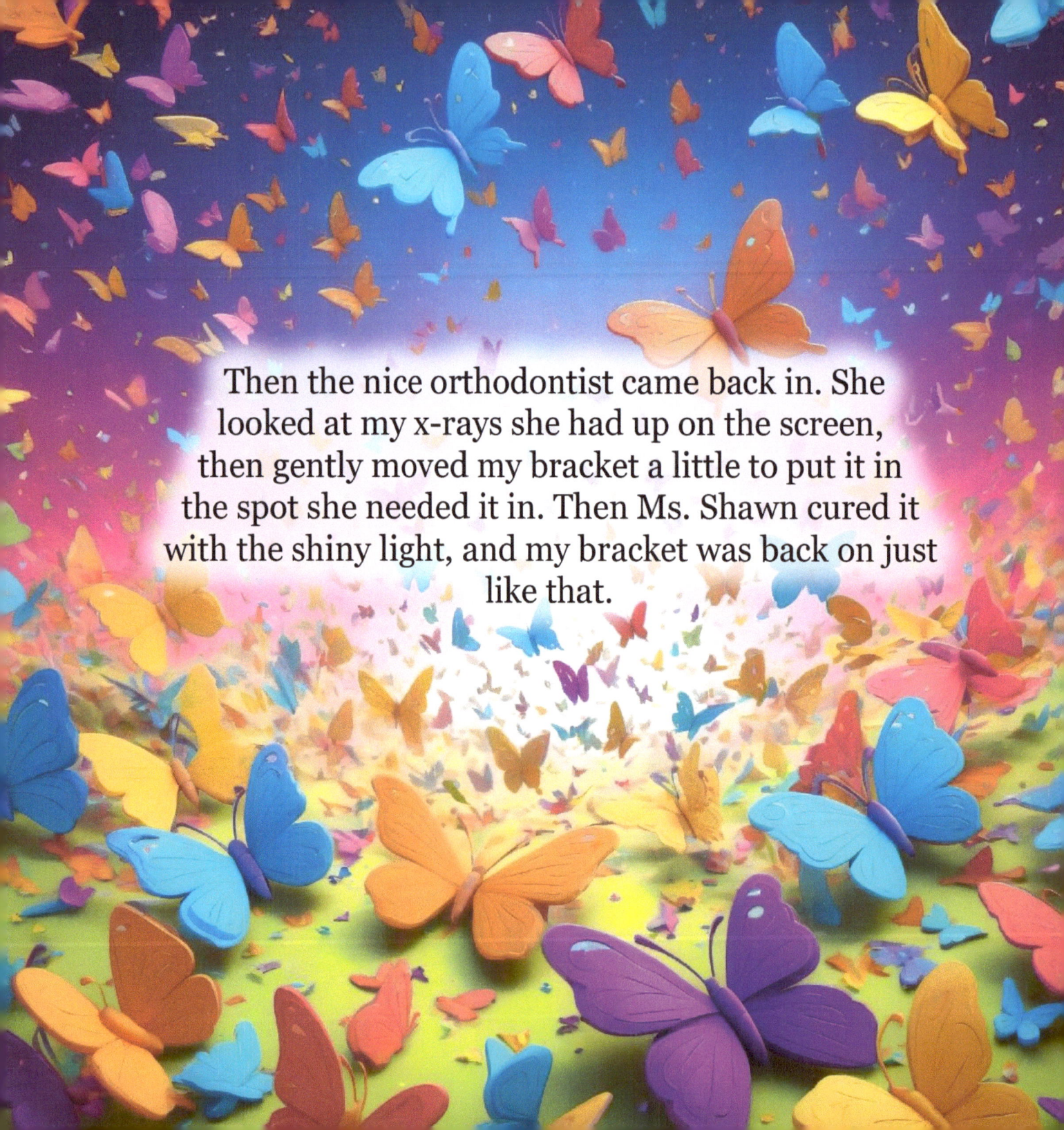

Then the nice orthodontist came back in. She looked at my x-rays she had up on the screen, then gently moved my bracket a little to put it in the spot she needed it in. Then Ms. Shawn cured it with the shiny light, and my bracket was back on just like that.

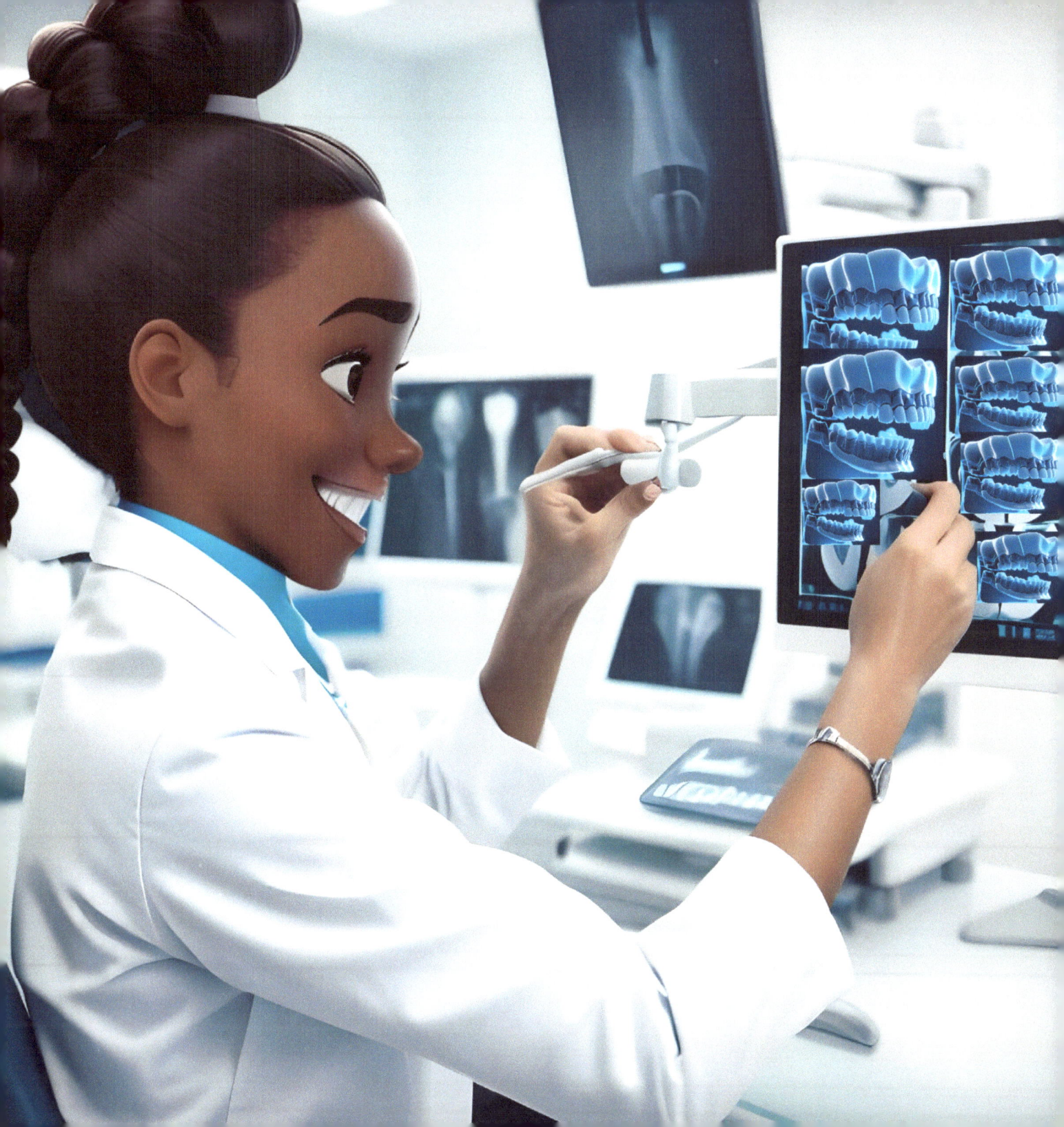

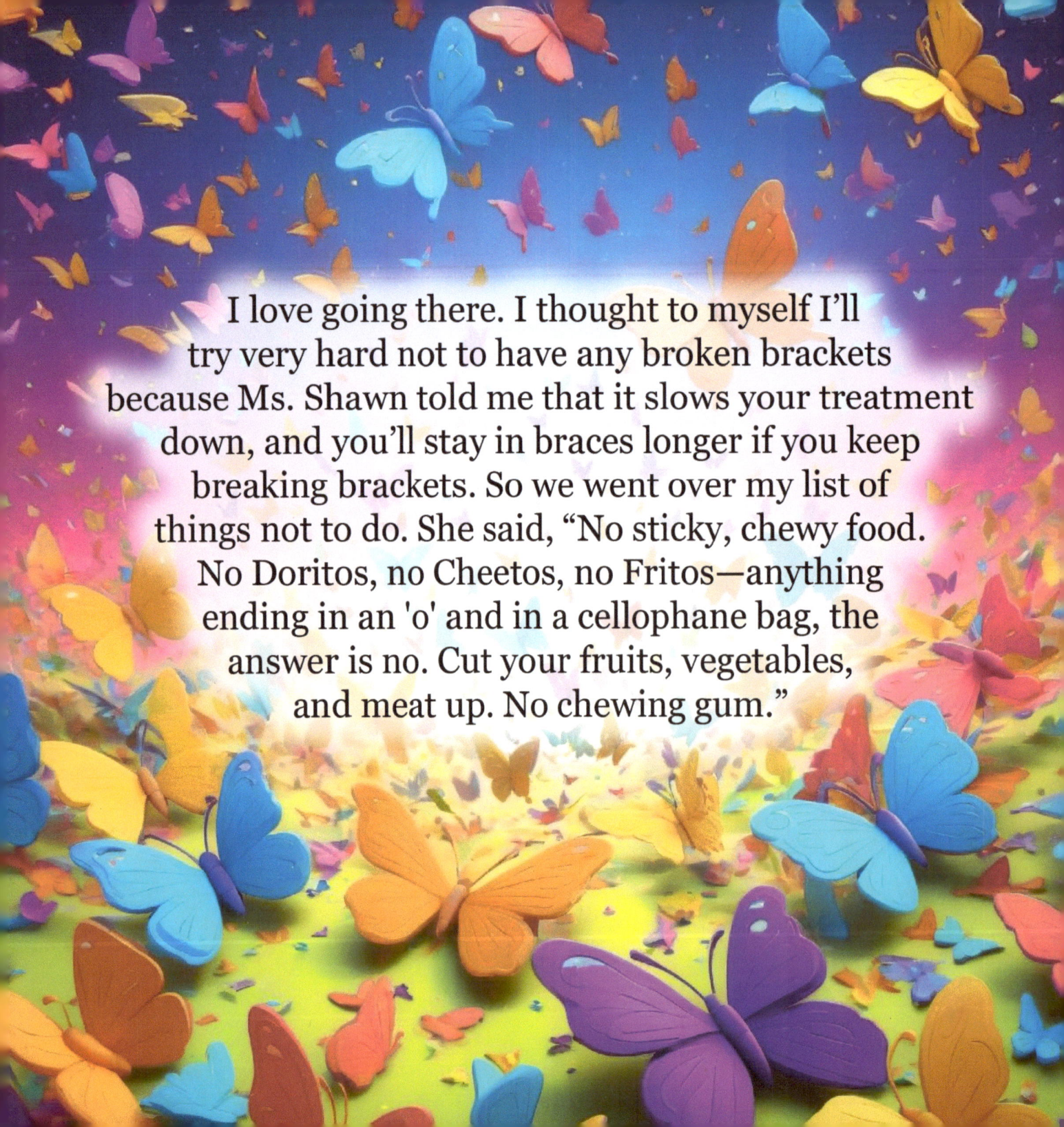

I love going there. I thought to myself I'll try very hard not to have any broken brackets because Ms. Shawn told me that it slows your treatment down, and you'll stay in braces longer if you keep breaking brackets. So we went over my list of things not to do. She said, "No sticky, chewy food. No Doritos, no Cheetos, no Fritos—anything ending in an 'o' and in a cellophane bag, the answer is no. Cut your fruits, vegetables, and meat up. No chewing gum."

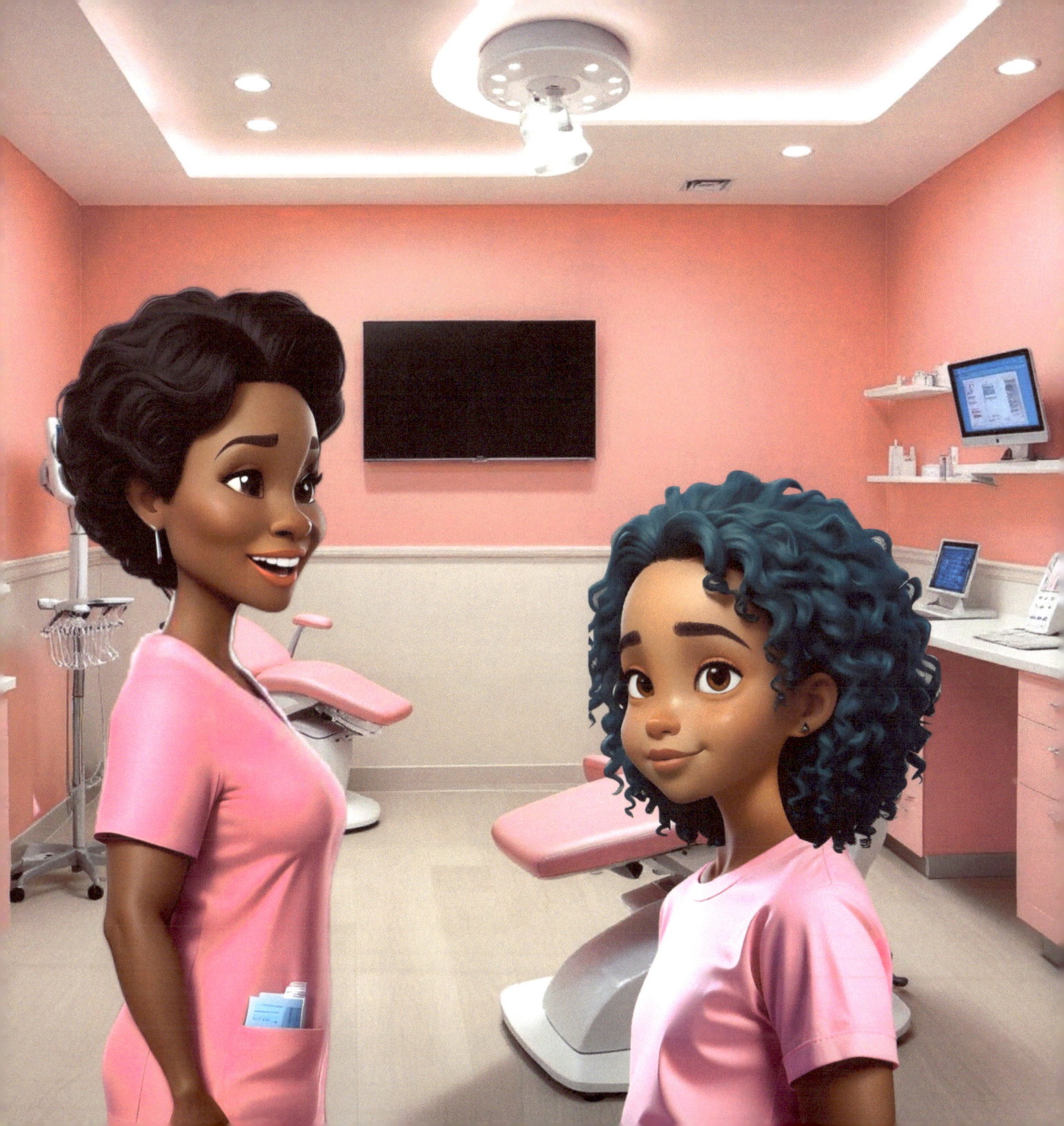

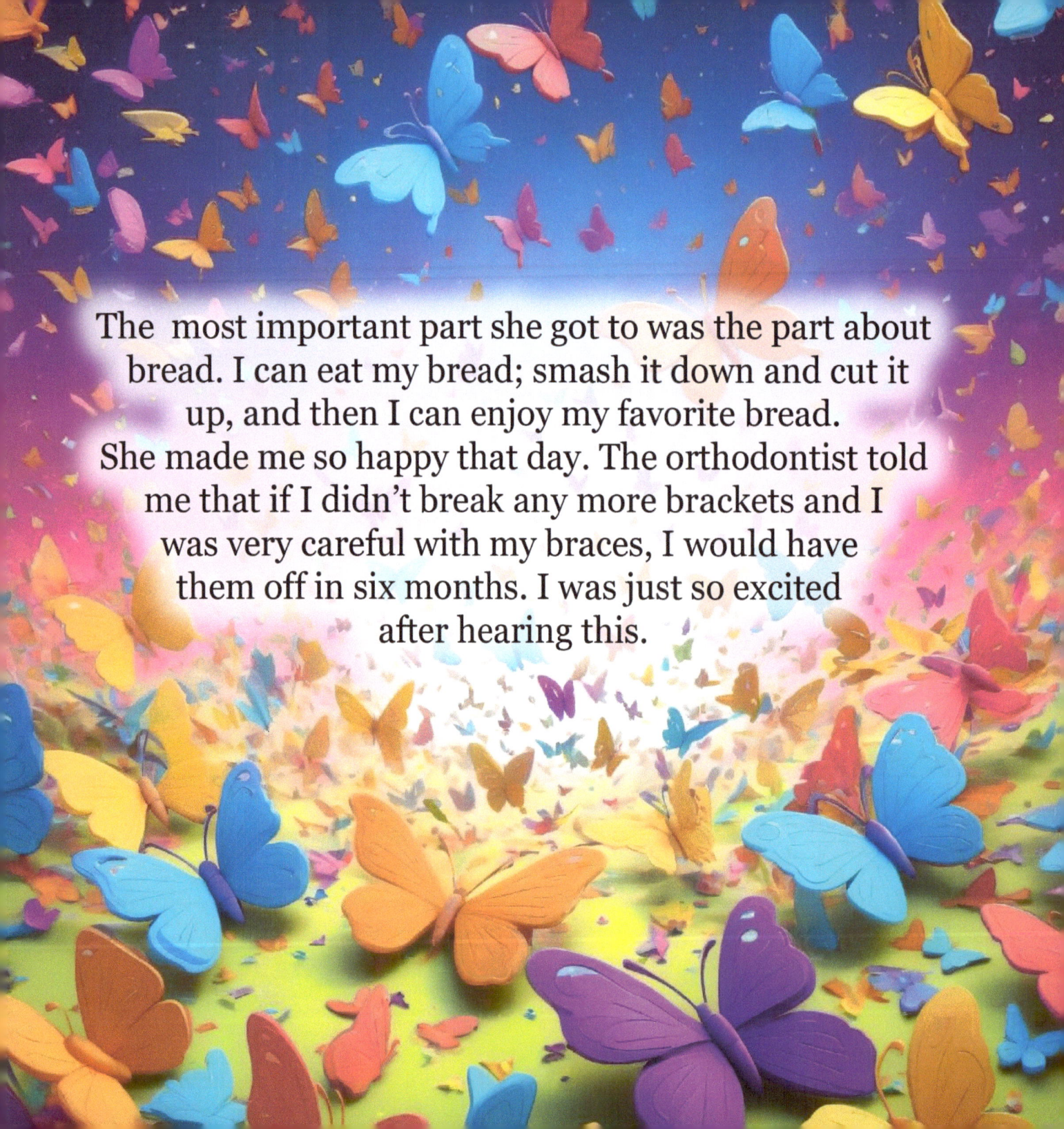

The most important part she got to was the part about
bread. I can eat my bread; smash it down and cut it
up, and then I can enjoy my favorite bread.
She made me so happy that day. The orthodontist told
me that if I didn't break any more brackets and I
was very careful with my braces, I would have
them off in six months. I was just so excited
after hearing this.

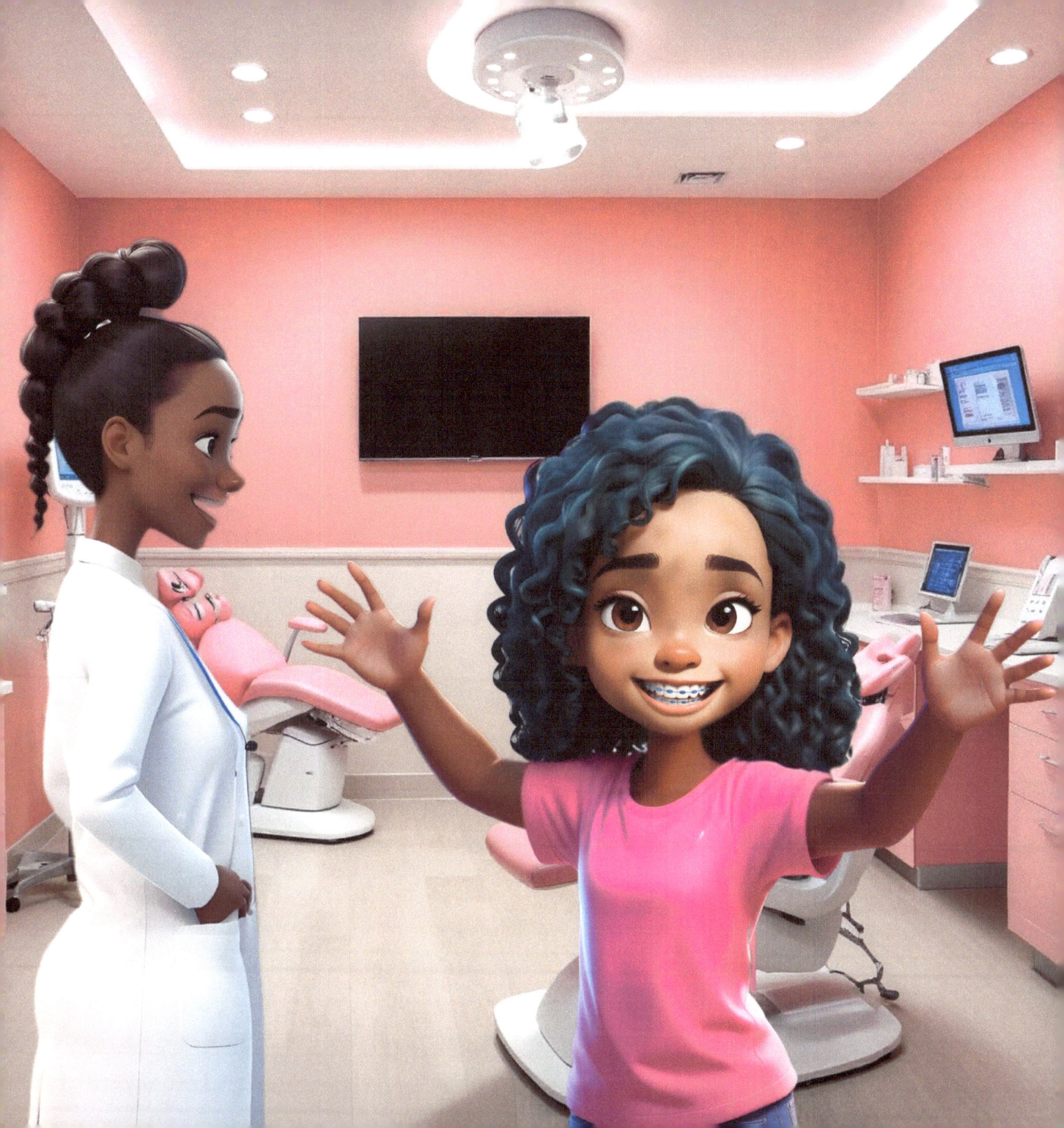

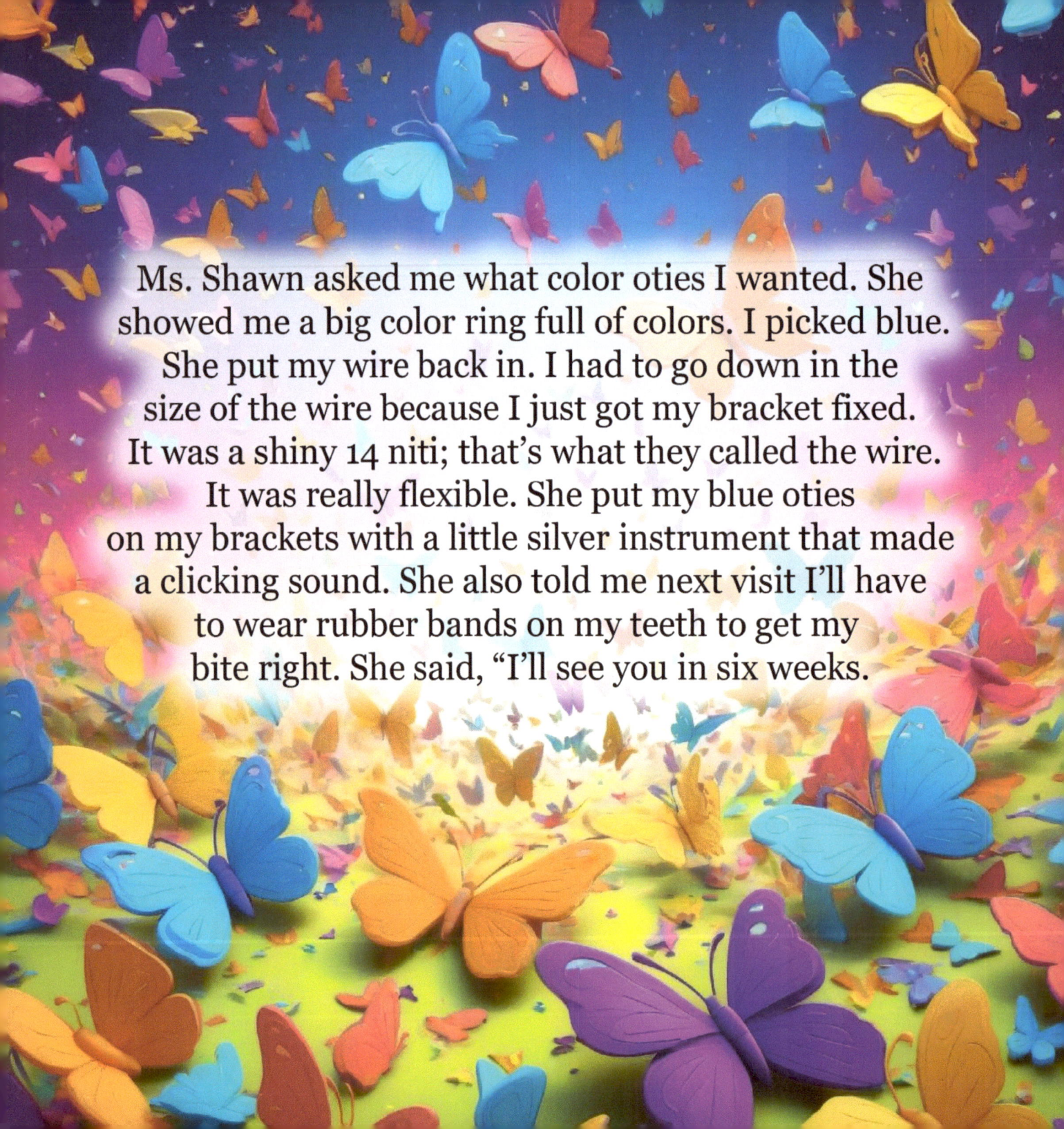

Ms. Shawn asked me what color oties I wanted. She showed me a big color ring full of colors. I picked blue. She put my wire back in. I had to go down in the size of the wire because I just got my bracket fixed. It was a shiny 14 niti; that's what they called the wire. It was really flexible. She put my blue oties on my brackets with a little silver instrument that made a clicking sound. She also told me next visit I'll have to wear rubber bands on my teeth to get my bite right. She said, "I'll see you in six weeks.

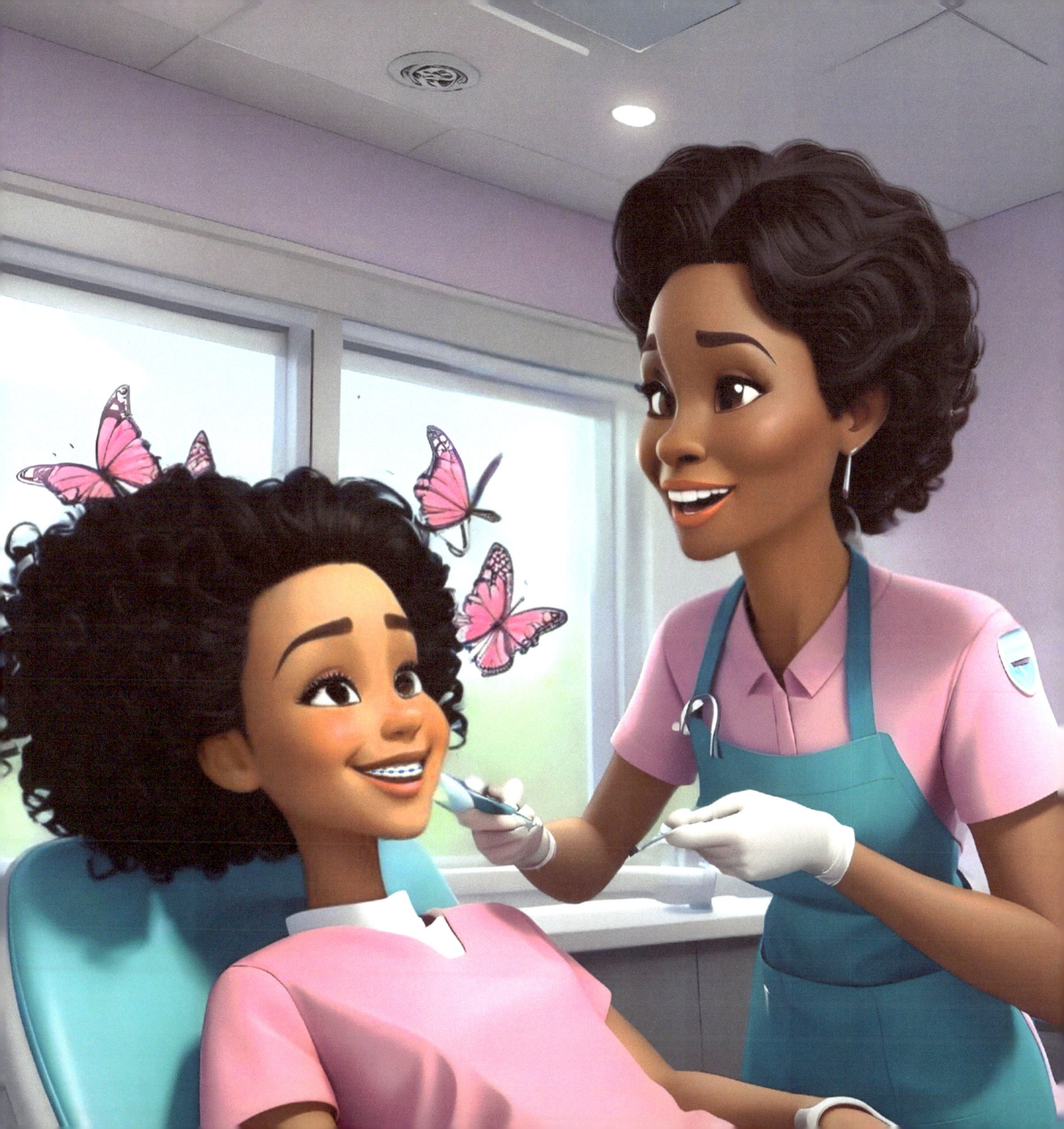

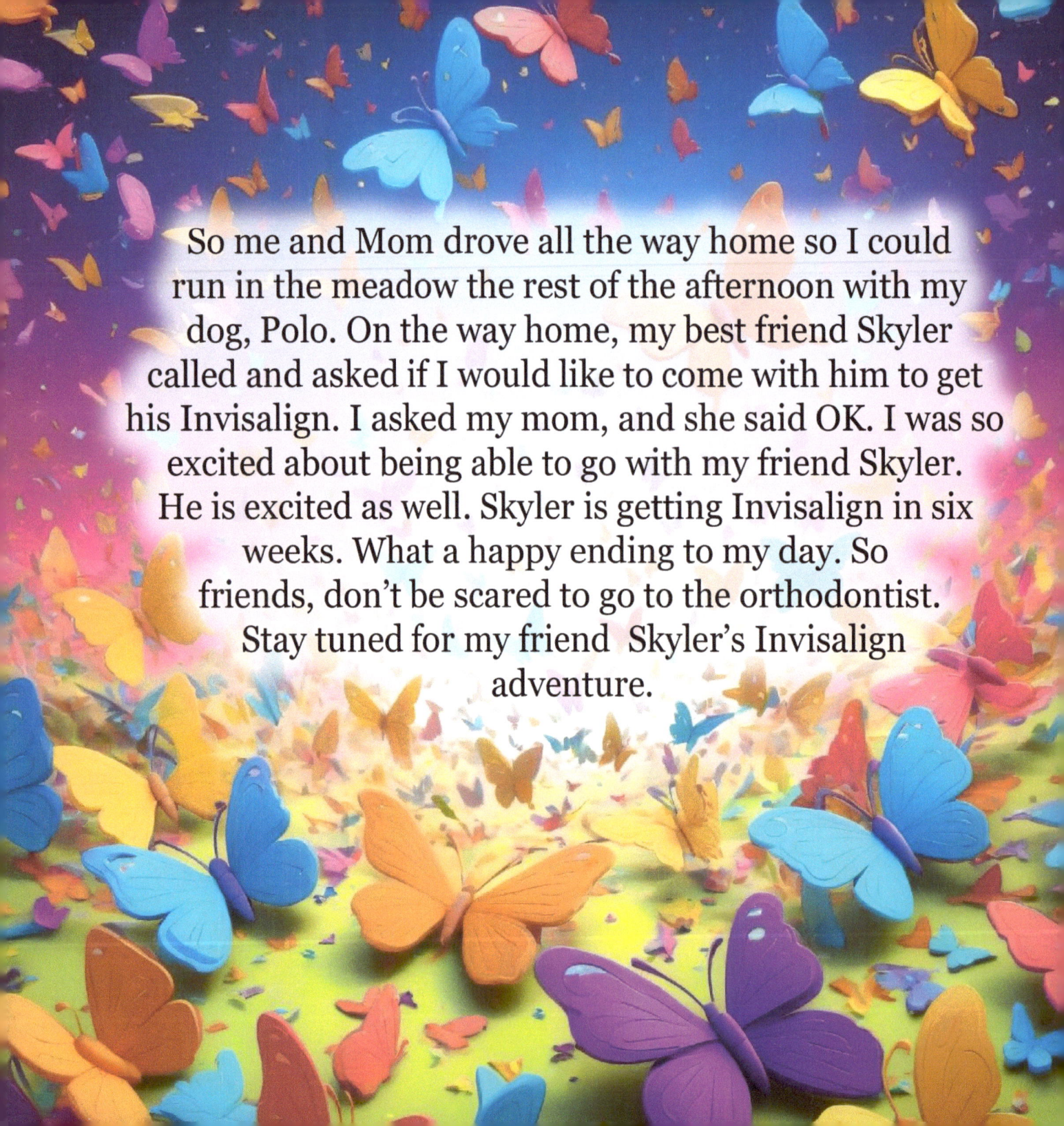

So me and Mom drove all the way home so I could run in the meadow the rest of the afternoon with my dog, Polo. On the way home, my best friend Skyler called and asked if I would like to come with him to get his Invisalign. I asked my mom, and she said OK. I was so excited about being able to go with my friend Skyler. He is excited as well. Skyler is getting Invisalign in six weeks. What a happy ending to my day. So friends, don't be scared to go to the orthodontist. Stay tuned for my friend Skyler's Invisalign adventure.

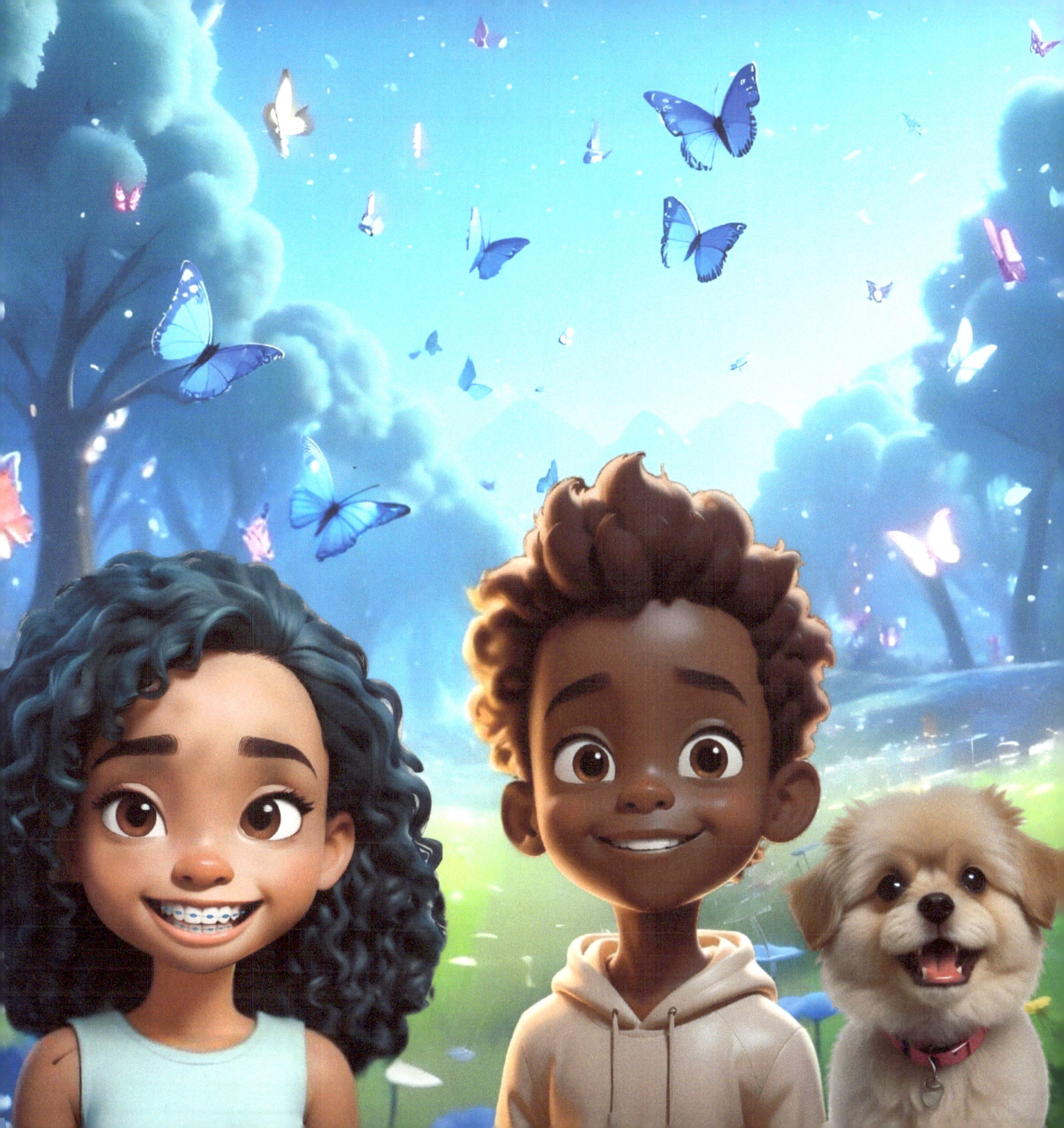